insomnia

ISBN: 979-8-9873496-1-8

Written, edited, and produced by Kiana Lin.

Cover design by Kiana Lin.

www.creativeinklin.com

For the sleepless ones, the aspiring souls,
For the tired and wakeful dreamers.

MOONRISE

It starts with a
Star that falls
And ends with
The rock that rises.

Glancing up,
A flash of disappearing brightness–
A sign as bare branches,
Looking alive as grasping hands,
Reach, stretch, to touch the last of the sunlight.

Dusk hardly falls
Before we rush to banish it back.
The natural order not to our liking,
We take matters into our own hands,
And look where it has brought us:
Harsh and false and exhausted
Light.

The unsettling nature of
Shadows
Is not their existence,
But the secrets they gather
Just outside the light.

Fell, fallen–
We describe dark,
Despicable,
Things by these words.
So why is it that we
Fall in love?

Leaves live many lives,
Don't you think? But all we know
How they shade, float, fall.

The smell of rain
Is a torturous thing–
Waiting for the first tears
To drop.

I sat alone to cry today.
But, instead of tears,
All that fell out were words.
I guess my storms only rain poetry.

Clouds are simply mist,
Yet a single one impacts
Even the bright sun.

Beauties to capture,
Nature slips through my fingers–
Moments lost, of course.

A slate, wiped clean–
It was always meant
To be temporary,
But did you think
Of this exact future?
The blankness,
With only a hint of what was,
And everything else:
Lost entirely to the past.

Always so busy
Looking ahead,
I missed the magic–
Slain and scattered–
Just behind.

Life on the precipice–
Mundane in nature–
Yet, even calloused fingers grow weary.
And you would question
My fatigue
At always being on the outer edges.

Have patience,
Be patient,
Wait patiently:
You hand out advice
As if you know
What I have accomplished,
See all that I have endured.
I have lived
A life of patience.
I am not *im*patient.
I am simply
Exhausted with it.

There was once a season
Where I loved puzzles.
Gave time and acquired joy
From the solving of problems,
The unraveling of difficulties.
A mind–once enamored with riddles–
Riddled and depleted now.

Exhaustion, how long
Until you are finally
Exhausted?

Too weary to be angry,
Too sad to let it go.

Fatigued and fatiguing
To be around:
I see the collision,
The incoming destruction,
But am too tired
Even to press the brake.

Hoping
Just so you can have an answer.
Hoping
It's anything else.

-justnotThatOneThingplease

My heart doesn't want
To work today.
It is heavy and heavier
For all it is
Absorbing and cleansing,
For me and everyone I meet.
My heart doesn't want to,
But it will work today.
It just won't be pumping out
To the wider world.

Everyone points out
The exits that are clearly marked,
Asking me if I see the fire.
They want me to escape for their comfort,
But they forget I am the firefighter
Who is meant to do battle
And be in the thick of it.
I may get burned, yes,
But that is what I signed up for:
The chance to dance in the flames,
And, also,
The realities of getting singed.

They all keep trying
To give me an out
I never asked for:
I know my options,
I know my limits,
But until I am no longer
Called this way,
Directed this way,
Held to the vows I
Spoke this way–
I will continue in
The way of love.

Where the road meets the sky–
It's always uphill.

I cannot conceive
Of an English word
That has such a capacity,
As much changeability, as
Ever.

-I Wonder If I Will Ever Fall Sleep?

MIDNIGHT

In many ways,
Death and I
Are of a like mind:
The granting of rest,
So hardfought,
So often denied.

How closely
Life and Death
Nestle together,
Until you can't tell
Where one begins
And the other ends.

Suspended between
Life and death–of course–aren't they
The most beautiful?

I've always hated limbo,
Been such a sore loser.
So
What must it say
About me,
That I would choose
Fire and suffering
Over endless,
Limitless,
In between?

A little shadow is beautiful.
A bit of shade is a haven.
In small doses, it's a gift.
But gathering darkness
Looms and oppresses–
Drowns even sound–
And leaves us
Stifled,
Caught.

Urgency and calm
Clash within–
Unsettled,
Imbalanced,
And I teeter
On the edge,
Fall into
The abyss of
Anxiety
For some unknown.

Not enough time,
The future too
Stretched,
Waiting for the elastic
To spring back and
Shorten,
So afraid I will pull until
I break.

Never is never quite as done
As I think–
Is always more unbearable
With my every utterance
Of the word.

It feels like exile,
But it's a choice.
And it's rending.
My ability to be healthy
Or yours?

It feels like exile,
But it's a choice.
And it's rending.
My ability to be healthy
Or yours?

Memories,
Echoes,
Left to suffuse the spaces–
A lingering presence in a place
Once called home,
But not this time.
More mine than others,
But I couldn't bring myself
To sing to those walls.
I left only tears–
The rooms were haunted enough
With raised voices.

Can I pick your brain
A moment?
Perhaps your answers
Will quiet
The questions eviscerating
My mind.

Hateful is my hope,
Because it comes bound up–
Packaged–in the sadness
Wrapped around you.

Tell me if you know me best.
Do you?
If I said to meet me at
My spot,
Would you know where
To go?
How could you, when I
Can't decide
And I'm alone, driving
In circles,
Wandering and then sitting in
The dark.

I'd like to think I know every you,
But I can't.
You assume you know every me,
But you won't.
I never can
And you never will.

Space can be terrifying
For those who already know–
For those who fear–
With what they will fill
The void.

It's easier to make
Ridiculous leaps
When you're already
Out on the farthest ledge.

Sliding down this hole,
Because these bruises and cuts
Are more tolerable than the aches
That ascension will bring.

More work than balancing–
Hovering on the edge–
Trying desperately to plunge and sink
Quietly into the deep.
And being drawn ever up,
Thrashing, back to safety.

Drowning,
My greatest fear,
And, yet–
I am deluded
By the deluge,
Find my comfort
In all the things
That keep me
From breathing deeply.

Swimming,
For all its smooth grace,
Is struggle.

Drowning,
For all its violent sorrow,
Is simple.

Rendered immobile by the
Creep of encroaching stone,
Cold and weighty and coarse.
No wonder we name the feeling of
Our greatest of fears as being
Petrified.

Overused,
Overheard,
Overwhelmed,
Over-edited–
Until I'm just
Over.

I am like paper–
Terrible and tearable–
Fleeting, useful, gone.

The words come
At the worst of times.
The poetry dries up
When I need it most.
My pen is full of ink,
But the paper is empty.
My mind is cluttered with thoughts,
But my lips are barren wastelands.

The older the books,
The more they weep–
Ink stains become the blood spots
To commemorate the graves of
The dead thoughts and dreams.

Heart,
Mind,
Soul–
Immortal words on fluttering pages,
Long after blood and bones
Disintegrate.

Dissipate,
Disperse,
Diffuse–
Words linked to one another,
Meanings so similar,
And connotations too distant.

I don't know
Why
The things I feel
Become
The words I can't say.

I have lived my life
Adhering to the timelines
Of others.
Coerced and manipulated,
Taken advantage of and violated
By the schedules and agendas
Of others.
And when I am tired,
In need of rest and to feel loved,
It is my tragedy that I only want
And require the time and attention
Of others.

The final day
We belonged to one another
Wasn't the last time
We said goodbye.
But I hate that I can't tell
Which hug was the end.

Drying eyes,
A muddled heart,
Yet my soul is lightening
As you depart.

Sometimes, I think
Shadows
Reveal even more than
Reflections.

Today feels like a day
To lose things.
A day to wander and
Wonder how to return.
A day to hide in the cracks,
Leak through the crevices,
Lie forgotten inside of couch cushions,
And contemplate if
I even want to become
Unlost.

I've lived by seeking patterns,
Following impressions,
And choosing intuition.
Yet I'm still learning the balance
Between impending disaster
And anxious wrongness.
One is deep and oppressive and pervasive.
The other is sharp and quick and pulsing.
One has helped me survive
And the other has almost ended me.

What I want most in living this life
Is actually quite simple:
It's simplicity–just that.
If life was a little,
How much more could it
Fit? Expanding
Until we
Can just
Be.

Everyone needs a place
Where there are no rules.
Mine is in the blank pages
And unassuming spaces
Where the ink hasn't
Yet found purchase.

Poetry is for the soul
As
Sun is for the skin–
Relished perfection or
Lingering pain.

Working so hard
To be seen,
Bringing my shadows
To life in the light.
But wraiths are creatures
Of the darkness
And I feel myself slithering
Back to black.
Which will be my downfall–
Moon or sun?

MOONSET

Your very first time
Or at your thousandth attempt,
Something new creeps in.

The emptiness that stewed and stifled
Before
Came on the back of a flurry, a commotion.
This hollowed space of opportunity–
Now
Fullness arrives on the wings of wind and rain.

So rarely am I without
Words.
And–if I am–just give me
Time,
Allow me the use of a blank
Page.

My worst moments
Have written my best lines.
The most ugly things
Have birthed my most beautiful words.
My terrible, broken parts
Gave life to a wondrous and full voice.

-Bittersweet Well

A thin-tipped pen
Shows your hand
In so many
Unintentional ways,
Shares more readily
The mistakes you
Wish to hide.
A fine pen
Reveals truths
You aren't yet
Prepared to face.

I don't write to distinguish myself,
To be a singularity.
I write to relate,
To use my words to find
Where you and I
Intersect–
Our shared experience.
I use these solitary activities
To find my community
And peace.

Pages
All in my handwriting,
Words
All of my own choosing,
Freedom–
All the worlds at my fingers.

Ink–
The only one to which
I've never
Had to apologize.

Is it poetry
If they're all so shortened?
Why else waste my words?

You don't look like a poet.
Of course not.
I'm just the poem.

Don't you think–if the eyes are windows
To the soul, then voices would be
Indicative of the heart?
And hearts, easily crushed,
Need medicine still.
So how to heal
The unseen
Hurting?
Sing.

A dream made tangible
Is life turned magic.

There is difference
Between an art and a mess–
It is intention.

Subtlety is a superpower–
Quiet, mysterious, and yet,
It holds such influence still.
What battles can't be won
With strength, force alone,
Only a touch–
Soft here, deft
There–can,
Will.

I posit:
We are never stuck,
Merely indecisive.

So sorry all the time,
But I don't feel the same.
I am not unburdened by life.
It gets difficult, of course.
I get sad, as we must.
I am tired like you,
But sorry to be alive?
I will always refuse.

You didn't ask to be born,
You didn't choose to be here–
Until you did.
And then you kept choosing,
Are still,
Again and again.
Your struggle and your decisions
Are noticed
And are worthy of pride.

-If You're Reading This . . .

Tears, once again,
But all I can ask,
All I can hope for:
That you are still.
Well and truly
Safe
And sound
And still.

Touch.
It was the first connection.
Breathing normal,
Heartbeat slow.
Simplicity became
More.

The changing was involuntary,
Almost as if–right now!–
We jumped, breathless and swaying
Back and forth,
And emerged still
Together in the pale light:
Hand-in-hand.

I looked back
As he leaned forward,
Staring, eyes lit up.
I swear, I can't explain it,
Lips unmoving,
But he spoke in a soft voice,
Just a whisper–
Just my name.

Hold my heart
Like a daydream–
Not so tight
That you squelch it,
Not so loose
That it slips away.

Enthrall me,
That my soul
May be home
And–
Even amongst the throng–
Find its way back.

If you're looking
For one last kiss,
Stay close.
A soft beam of light,
Someone moving,
A whisper:
I love doing this.
This time–
Just quietly right.

A moonset shrouded in grey morning,
Rain covering, inhibiting our sight,
But–when artificial meets natural–
The world dazzles still,
Dressed in red-sequined, blurred splendor.

The first beam of sunlight belongs to me.
I hold her captive as long as
Sunshine warmth stays settled into my skin,
Her magic seeping into my veins,
Carrying solar flares to my heart,
Vitality dispersed in golden rays.
Still, insomnia is a taste that lingers,
The proof not so easily washed away.

Skeletal trees
Kicking up a blur of sounds–
Just in time–
With the sun
Scurrying past
To wake the world,
Her creeping warmth
Bringing drowsiness
At last.

And finally, rest arrives,
For aspiring souls need sleep.
All the better to dream, then
Rule the waking world.

Tantalized with beginnings–
Those things that are actually endings.

ABOUT THE AUTHOR

Ever since she was a child, Kiana Lin has had a love of words. From her first made up phrase (to fit her stubborn idea) to learning to read (out of a spiteful need for independence), she took in every bit of wordplay and storytelling craft that she could. Then, one summer, a creative writing assignment led to a late brainstorming session in her aunt and uncle's kitchen. That one night sparked the desire to create something she would enjoy reading for herself.

And then she never stopped.

insomniac is Kiana Lin's sixth full-length work, and she is–of course–still writing! For her social media and to learn more, visit her website:

www.creativeinklin.com